SPARKY AND ME II

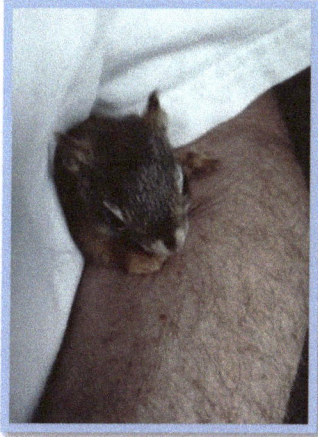

More Adventures
with a
Delightful Red Squirrel
(Where will it end?)

Other books by Richard K. Meissner

Sparky and Me: Adventures with a Baby Red Squirrel

Sparky and Me II

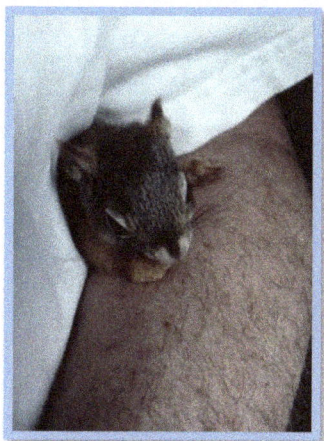

More Adventures
with a
Baby Red Squirrel
(Where will it end?)

Richard K. Meissner

Henschel
HAUS
www.henschelHAUSbooks.com

Milwaukee, Wisconsin

Published by
HenschelHAUS Publishing, Inc.
Milwaukee, Wisconsin
www.HenschelHAUSbooks.com

Quantity discounts available.

ISBN: 978-1-59598-906-2
E-ISBN: 978-1-59598-907-9
Library of Congress Control Number: 2022936493

Printed in the United States of America.

Thank you to the
Editorial Advisors
Judy Reinders, Cindy Musbach
& Hildegard Meissner

In memory of
Joanne Minessale
The second-grade teacher, friend, and neighbor
who inspired me to write this book.
(October 29, 1943 — August 18, 2021)

Table of Contents

Prelude and Photographs 1

1. Brrrrrrr! What a Winter! 5
2. Spring is Finally Here 9
3. Morning Routine 11
4. Spring Observations 16
5. Squirrel House Condo............................19
6. Always a Happy Little Squirrel 22
7. Sparky has a Girlfriend, I Think 26
8. More Red Squirrels—The Confusion Begins..........29
9. Sparky's Skin Disease Gets Worse....................33
10. Surprise! Five Baby Red Squirrels! 36
11. Confusion Resolved 40
12. One Happy Family—Little Sparks Everywhere!.....45
13. The Little Sparks Grow Up Fast 53
14. Sparky, It's Time to Reclaim My Boat!................58
15. Why Is My Yard so Quiet? 60

Fun Photos 65
Closing Remarks from the Author................69
References and Credits 70
About the Author 73

Sparky, 10 weeks old

Prelude

Sparky and Me, Book 1, was a light-hearted story about a human mother (Richard), who raised a baby red squirrel (Sparky). They were an odd couple from the beginning, but they became friends. Once Sparky matured, natural instincts called him back to nature.

Sparky continued to hang around and made a winter home in the bottom of Richard's boat. This was a surprise to Richard, but he did not have the heart to kick Sparky out, since Sparky had already stored his winter food cache in the boat.

Therefore, the story about Sparky & Me never seems to end. Again, laugh along with Sparky, the baby red squirrel, in the following tale. The journey will entertain you. The combined books describe the adventures of an orphaned infant red squirrel who achieves adulthood in a matter of months.

Fall 2020

Sparky preparing for winter.

08:47AM 11

Winter 2021

Sparky living in an aluminum boat.

02:46PM 01/20/2021

1

Brrrrrrr! What a Winter!

This was Sparky's first winter, and what a winter it was. Sparky was all by himself with nobody to teach him how to survive, since Sparky did not have a mother and father. How did Sparky know he needed to collect and store a food cache of hickory nuts? How did he stay warm during those freezing cold winter nights outside? Did he eat snow for water? Did he even know what snow was?

As a surrogate mother, I did not and could not teach him any of these things. All I could do was make sure he had some extra almonds and pinecones to eat, and water to drink. The water froze within minutes of putting it outside. I did this daily, and fortunately, there were no other animals around to steal the food, except for a mouse that was also living in the boat along with Sparky.

Snow, snow, and more snow! What was Sparky to do? All he could do was poke his head out, look around, grab some almonds, and crawl back into his small hole. The snow kept getting deeper, and the hole continued to get smaller. Some days the hole was completely covered in snow.

Throughout the winter, I knew it was Sparky who was living in my boat because I put blue fleece strips on the back of the boat, and numerous videos showed him grabbing the fleece. He would then carry them to his den.

> *Winters in Wisconsin can be very cold for a period of three to four months. It usually starts to snow in December and melts in March.*

What other red squirrel would know what to do with the blue fleece strips?

For four months, Sparky lived in the bottom of an aluminum fishing boat in freezing weather. He ate nothing but his food cache of hickory nuts, and some almonds, sunflower seeds, and seeds from pinecones, which I provided to him. I believe he ate snow for water. Now, that is impressive! What a boring four months..., sleep, poke your head out, look around, and crawl back into your den. Fortunately, Sparky loved to eat almonds, which are high in fat. The extra fat layer on his body probably kept him alive.

Tree squirrels do not hibernate. They nest in their den and are fully functional, although not very active. They sleep a lot to pass the time, similar to humans. But, for the most part they are eating, walking, running, climbing, and searching for more food beneath the snow. They rely on sheltered nests or dens, fat reserves, and stored food to survive the long, cold winter. Their natural instincts allow them to know winter is coming by the length of day changes. Squirrels can survive 5 to 8 days without food but need water daily.

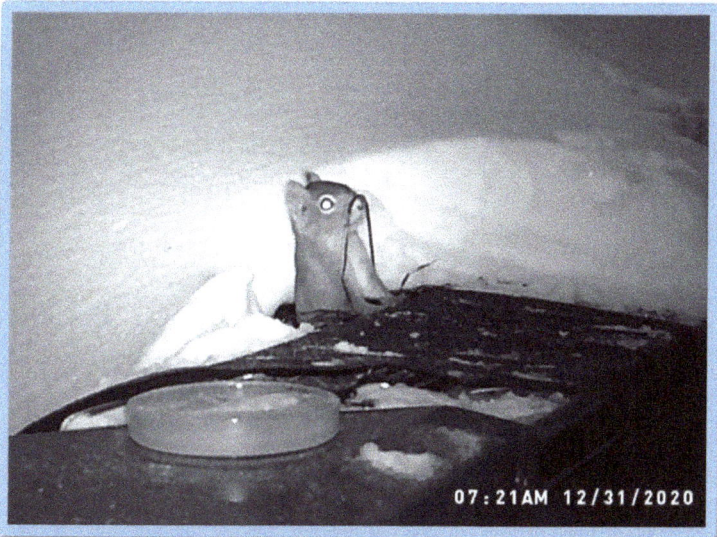

07:21AM 12/31/2020

Sparky could have chosen to live in my house, but natural instincts told him that he belonged outdoors.

Unless they are used to living in the cold, most people couldn't survive a single night. There are no TVs, cell phones, hot cooked meals, showers or toilets.

During the winter of 2021, there was a stretch of weather when the temperature was below zero for a period of three weeks straight—nothing but cold, cold, cold.

From day one, Sparky had a strong desire to survive. He again proved that to me through that winter. I personally did not think he would make it.

I consider this an unbelievable feat of survival. Sparky was maybe two times the size of a chipmunk, at best. It would not take long for Old Man Frost to freeze Sparky into an ice cube.

If you were a squirrel like Sparky, how do you think you'd survive during the cold winter months outdoors?

2
Spring is Finally Here

Ah! Spring is in the air, and Sparky decided to venture out from his den.

"My tail!, My tail!" said Sparky.

"Did I freeze my tail off?"

"Oh thank goodness, there it is."

But, "EEEEk! It is bright orange. What happened to my tail?," Sparky wondered.

It was a ridiculously cold winter. Snow was everywhere. It was deep, and it never seemed to melt. For Sparky, it was incredibly boring. All Sparky could do was sleep and eat in the deep, dark bilge of the boat. The snow was too soft and too deep to run in, and Sparky was an easy target for a hawk or eagle in the white snow. Sparky probably thought he was going to freeze to death. It was

cold, very cold. And to Sparky's surprise, the majority of his hickory nuts had worms in them. There was no heat or electricity in the dark bottom of the boat. But luckily for Sparky, the man (Richard) who lived in the big house gave him almonds throughout the winter months.

"EEEEK," said Sparky. "How did I get so fat?"

And, "I now have hair tufts on the top of my ears. What happened to me?" wondered Sparky.

"But, ah! That sun feels good."

It was March and Sparky was now eleven months old. He had made it through his first winter. It was evident that he was excited to feel the warmth of spring. He was able to once again jump from tree to tree, run on the ground, check out all of the tree holes, mingle with his forest friends, and find and hide nuts.

To Sparky, spring was heaven, and his only thoughts were, "I'm back! What is to eat?"

Sparky still had endless energy and could jump to no end.

3
Morning Routine

In the early morning hours of each day, the trees came alive with all of the forest animals, including, crows, sparrows, squirrels, rabbits, and chipmunks. However, by 10:00 a.m., they all seemed to disappear, including Sparky. I guess it was nap time when their bellies were full.

In the evening around 6:00 p.m., the activity picked up again. Every animal was looking for food again. This lasted until sunset.

During the month of April, I continued to feed Sparky almonds, sunflower seeds, and water in the early morning, but his wake-up time seemed to have shifted slightly this year. I did not see him for breakfast until 8 or 8:30 a.m. I was fine with his later wake-up time, but every time I put food out, the gray squirrels, various birds, and chipmunks would eat the nuts before he got there.

My solution became a routine of placing half of the nuts and seeds on the back of the boat and the other half

What is your favorite season of the year?

on the front porch of the squirrel tree house. Then I would knock on the side of the boat, and say, "Sparky, get up. It's breakfast time."

Like clockwork and within ten minutes, Sparky would appear ready and eager to eat. In the evening, it was just the opposite. I would see Sparky waiting in the trees with a glare in his eye. *"Where is that nut guy? What... no nuts? Come on... give me, give me, give me some nuts."*

For fun, I decided to give Sparky a one-year birthday party. Guess what I gave him? *Whipped cream!*

He loved it, and he acted as goofy as he had as a baby twelve months earlier.

The snow has finally melted, which allowed Sparky to once again hide his nuts or seeds. It was a fun process to watch, though I could never understand how he chose

his hiding places. Sometimes he traveled fifty yards to bury or hide a nut, and at other times, it was just at the base of his tree in the dirt or grass. When the hiding place was the grass, he ran down his tree at lightning speed, jumped on the grass, hopped around a little bit, dug a hole with his front feet, put the nut in place, and fluffed the dirt or grass over the top. He was done in seconds.

In Sparky's mind, I am sure he felt like he did an excellent job at burying the nut, but in reality, the nut was barely hidden. I could see them when I walked on the grass or looked at a fork in the tree branch.

How do you think squirrels remember where they hid their nuts?

What an Unusual Character! (Referring to Sparky, of course!)

Regardless, it was an enjoyable morning routine for me to watch while eating my breakfast.

On another morning, I decided to place some whipped cream up in the Sparky tree house to see if other squirrels liked it as well. As usual, the gray squirrels stopped by for some sunflower seeds, but they just walked through the whipped cream and made a mess. They did not even taste it.

Once Sparky showed up, he went all in and began to eat it just like he always did. However, this time he ate too

much. I did not see him the next day. He might have been recovering from a belly ache.

Neighbors kept asking me if Sparky was still around. I would say, "Yes, just look for this little orange high speed race car hopping through your yard. He is faster than last year."

Sparky had matured from fast, to faster, and now he was the fastest critter in my yard. It was like watching one of those super-hero movie figures race from one city street to another city street in the blink of an eye.

Neighbors also asked me how I knew this was Sparky. I would say, "I only have one red squirrel in my yard." and, "What other red squirrel eats whipped cream? What other red squirrel steals and hides blue fleece strips in tree holes?"

After six long months of Sparky being away from me, it appeared that his natural instincts seem to have softened slightly. Maybe it was the cold, lonely winter that created the change. I did not know. But, on several occasions, Sparky would jump into the tree and come within four feet of me as I placed food out.

On other occasions, he would be in the tree and let me get within twelve inches from him when I placed food out. Both were big changes in his behavior. I was once again tolerable to Sparky.

I would say Sparky did all of the following during the short time we have been living on the same property.

In general, wild animals are unpredictable. Sometimes they teach you, comfort you, show you affection, scare you, and impress you.

Just a morning stretch.

4
Spring Observations

It was now the month of May, and I was once again eating an early-morning breakfast on my front porch. Suddenly, out of the corner of my eye, I noticed a dark, blue bird flying around in the tall grass, then another, and another. Strangely, they always seemed to disappear behind this tree. I put my breakfast down and I walked over to the tree where I thought the dark blue birds had landed.

To my surprise, all I could see was a pile of blue fleece strips. I looked up and sure enough, it was Sparky removing the blue fleece strips from a tree hole. Last summer, I had watched him hide the blue fleece strips in the same hole.

One after another, Sparky kept throwing these blue fleece strips out of this hole. Between each strip, he just stared at me and continued on with the job at hand. As I scratched my head, I just had to say, "Sparky, what are you doing?"

In total, there were about a dozen blue fleece strips on the ground, and they were extremely dirty. I guess Sparky was either doing some spring cleaning, or he was looking for some buried food. I had no idea.

I continued to watch Sparky for a few minutes and decided that I should throw the fleece strips away. When I was finished, I placed some almonds in the squirrel tree house. Instantaneously, Sparky jumped tree to tree towards me, but he stopped three feet short. Again, the conflict between natural instincts versus visiting with an old friend confused Sparky. When I climbed down from the tree, Sparky went straight for the nuts.

The trees now had leaves on them, which provided camouflage for many animals. Day after day, the forest activity came alive every morning. The robins, blackbirds, sparrows, cardinals, blue jays, and crows flew around in a dizzying flight plan, all looking for food.

The chipmunks cruised the ground and trees like they were in a race. Once they found food, their mouth and cheeks acted like vacuum cleaners. And, off they went with their cheeks full.

The gray squirrels appeared to be in charge of the forest. They controlled the larger food sources…until oddly enough, Sparky came along. Nobody could touch the food in his squirrel tree house except for Sparky. He would chase the gray squirrels away.

There was another thing I noticed this past year, but I never gave it much thought. There always seemed to be a lot of little, green, leafy twigs lying on my lawn. I thought the wind had just knocked them down. But no, it was Sparky.

It seems that squirrels do not like any intruding obstacles in their way when racing through the trees. So, they clip the twigs off.

By chance, I was watching Sparky dash through the trees, and I noticed these little, green, leafy twigs falling to the ground after he cruised through his custom-built race track. It was interesting to watch because Sparky did not even stop to clip the twigs off. He would run and clip in

Snip! Snip! Snip!

one easy step as if he had an electric saw attached to his head.

I thought to myself, "What a clever concept." I never knew this before.

In winter, Sparky's head had acted like a snow plow to clear all of the snow from the branches.

5
Squirrel House Condo

For the last seven months, I had been thinking about a method to remove Sparky from my boat. I knew some people would say I was nuts for letting him nest in my boat, but again, I just could not get myself to kick him out unless he had some place to go.

It was now the middle of May, so I built a squirrel house condo. My thought was that maybe Sparky would like the squirrel house condo better than the boat and would just move on his own.

Off and on, I spent about three weeks designing and building the squirrel house condo. I worked on it rather slowly and during the construction process, I always placed almonds on each floor so Sparky would get used to a new enclosure/structure.

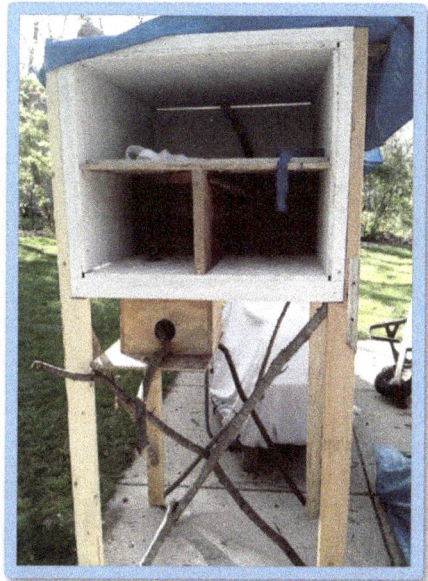

Again, I used the knowledge I had gained last summer from what Sparky appeared to like and not like. I designed the condo to be three levels with multiple rooms placed in a maze-like format. I included peep holes with screens on the sides. It also had an open attic area. The total size was about three feet square. It stood four feet off the ground and was about eight feet tall at the tip of the roof.

I used old buckthorn branches on the inside and outside of the house for a quick race track throughout. This time, I even insulated it...*crazy, crazy, crazy*.

I made the squirrel house condo rather big, since Sparky seemed to like using the rather large boat as a home last winter. Funny thought was that last year everyone told me that the squirrel tree house I made was too big for a little squirrel, but BOY!, were they wrong.

Well, as you guessed, things never seem to go the way you intend when dealing with Sparky. I noticed that

over the next two weeks, all of the nuts would disappear. I thought, "Great, Sparky was already getting used to the squirrel house condo." That was the wrong assumption. On purpose, I left the front door off the squirrel house condo so Sparky would get used to it quicker and not feel trapped inside of a cage.

One afternoon, I walked out my front door to look at the squirrel house condo and out flew a blue jay with an almond in its mouth.

I thought, "This is incredible! Is there any animal that I do not attract?"

Therefore, I put a front door on the condo, but I left it open slightly for light to get in. I also put some side curtains on the open attic area, because the blue jay would still enter the attic.

Sure enough, within days the chipmunks learned how to run through the rather complicated floorplan design and grab the nuts. I outsmarted the blue jay, but I still couldn't outsmart the chipmunks.

Later, I moved the squirrel house condo in the trees next to the front of the boat and placed a large buckthorn branch as a bridge to a large tree next to the boat for easy squirrel access. Soon, I would reclaim my boat, since I was not sure whether Sparky even lived in it anymore.

> *Would you be able to kick Sparky out of the boat in the middle of winter? How would you remove Sparky from the boat?*

6

Always a Happy Little Squirrel

Typically, I saw Sparky once or twice a day. However, on several occasions, Sparky would not appear for a day or two. When Sparky did return, he always seemed to be very happy and giddy. On several occasions, Sparky even put on a personal show for me. He would find some small tree branches about six to eight feet from me and start to jump and dance through the branches.

I'm not sure what he was trying to tell me, but he would stop, look at me, and do it again. The show only lasted two to three minutes. It was interesting to watch.

After the show, it was all about almonds and sunflower seeds. Sparky would watch where I put the nuts and seeds, and waited for me to leave before he began to eat. In his mind, I could not be in his tree or near his boat before he began to eat.

Later, I wondered if maybe Sparky was trying to tell me something with his happy dance. Had Sparky found a girlfriend? Maybe Sparky found his mother and father? What made Sparky disappear for a day or two and come back all happy and giddy? I did not know.

A few times, Sparky broke his natural instinct rules and came within one foot of me. The previous summer, it had been unconditional love; he would jump on me whenever food was around. This summer, I was not sure what it was. It appeared to be more like, *"Feed me!"* *"Where is my food?"* *"You're late!"*

I could usually tell when he thought I was late. Sparky would run around the tree that had the squirrel tree house, and he would stare at me. Does that sound like a teenager?

Sparky became an expert at chasing chipmunks from the tree as well. When the chase was on, it looked like an upside down race to see who got to the ground first. They were so fast that their little feet made a chattering noise on the bark.

However, happiness doesn't last forever. By the middle of May, I noticed a rash on Sparky's back shoulders after reviewing some of the trail cam photographs. This scared me a little, and I thought for sure

Sparky was going to have a very short life if he picked up some type of skin disease. I was not sure what to do.

Also in mid-May, I was eating dinner on my front porch. I noticed Sparky in the trees so I placed almonds on the squirrel tree house. Like always, Sparky came and sat in the attic of the squirrel tree house to eat some nuts. Out of nowhere, a blue jay landed on the attic of the squirrel

tree house and grabbed the nut from Sparky's front feet. Sparky ran under the roof and into the squirrel tree house. I realized this food thing was becoming impossible. The blue jay kept coming back to grab more. He even went into the attic of the squirrel tree house to steal more nuts.

So I now had to place curtains on the front and back of the squirrel tree house to slow down other birds and animals. These helped a little.

I still do not know how to feed Sparky without other animals stealing the food. Do you have any ideas?

7

Sparky has a Girlfriend, I Think

I was not sure who was chasing who, but two red squirrels were leaping from branch to branch about fifteen feet apart. The lead squirrel was making a loud screeching noise. I never heard that type of noise from Sparky before so I assumed that Sparky was chasing the other squirrel, but I was not sure. Sparky may have been protecting his territory, gotten into a fight with another squirrel, or had a new girlfriend (most likely). Regardless, they chased each other for as far as I could see. I didn't know for sure, but maybe Sparky was a neighborhood bully.

The next day, the same thing happened. Two red squirrels chased each other with the lead squirrel screeching "*Jeet, Jeet, Jeet! Jeet, Jeet, Jeet!*" It must have been a girlfriend. But, who was chasing who?

Ah! And there was that blue jay again. Without hesitation, he went through the attic curtain of the squirrel tree house and grabbed the almonds. You could always tell when the blue jay was around since the sparrows would dive bomb the blue jay to scare him off. It was a busy front yard when you took the time to watch and listen. It seemed like certain animals were always fighting for food.

And then, there was Sparky. He would do his danger dance with *"ERRRT, ERRRT, ERRRT!"* whenever another squirrel, including his girlfriend, disturbed his meal time. When Sparky ate, he did not want to be disturbed. I think that was what had started the high-speed chase through the trees with his girlfriend. She would wiggle in for a bite and off they would go on a loud, screeching chase.

Sparky's girlfriend was a talker. She had numerous sounds I had never heard before. Some of the sounds included:

- *"Urm, Urm, Urm, Urm, Urm"* with a downward tone like she was crying.
- *"Dong-a-Dong, Dong-a-Dong, Dong-a-Dong"* with a low-pitched sound
- *"Eat-Eat, Eat-Eat, Eat-Eat!"* with a high-pitched sound
- *"Girggle, Girggle, Girggle"* with a medium tone
- *"Bddddddddddddd"* with a low-pitched tongue roll (similar to the sound of a woodpecker, but softer)
- *"Beeeeeeeeeeee"* with a high-pitched tongue roll
- *"Brrrrrrrrrrrrrrrrr"* with a medium-pitched tongue roll
- *"Chip, Chip, Chip"* similar to a bird chirp

Let's face it, to humans, this all sounds like gibberish. Personally, I had no idea what the squirrels were saying.

Chipmunks, on the other hand, are famous for their repetitive *"Clucking"* noise. This means there's a hawk or other aerial predator in the area.

Whenever I saw Sparky and his girlfriend running through the treetops, they reminded me of Spiderman or Tarzan. Their routine was jump, grab, swing, and catch the next branch, followed by numerous other jumps, grabs, swings, and catch the next branch. It was pretty amazing to watch, especially when there were two red squirrels chasing each other at high speed while making all of those funny noises.

Every time I tried to imitate the squirrels with *"Brrrrrrrrrrrrrrrr,"* they became frightened. Obviously, I was unable to speak their language. I was very disappointed in myself.

> *With practice, do you think you could learn how to speak like a squirrel? What would you say?*

8

More Red Squirrels—
The Confusion Begins

It was now early June, and from a distance, I observed two red squirrels dance around a tree right next to Sparky's boat and the squirrel house condo. They were just chasing each other up and down, and around and around. They made no noises whatsoever. This went on for about twenty minutes, and then, they were gone.

At the same time, Sparky was eating sunflower seeds in the bird feeder about twenty feet away. For some reason, the two red squirrels did not seem to bother Sparky. He just kept eating. I asked myself, "Were the

Helloooooo???

two red squirrels potential girlfriends, or just friends? Who were these two red squirrels?"

That same day, I came home late in the evening. I wondered if Sparky was nearby, or was he out playing with his friends? As usual, I grabbed some almonds and walked through the front yard, calling Sparky's name. I really did not expect to see Sparky, but within minutes, I heard *"Gurgle, Gurgle, Gurgle."*

At first, I thought it was Sparky's talkative girlfriend, but no, it was Sparky. He came to me with his usual jumping and swinging routine through the treetops. Friends are always happy to see friends, so it did not take long for me to climb the ladder next to his tree and put almonds in the attic of his squirrel tree house. As soon as I climbed down the tree, Sparky jumped right into the attic of the squirrel tree house and began to eat the nuts.

I actually believe Sparky's *"Gurgle, Gurgle, Gurgle"* meant he was happy to see me. Or, as an alternative, he was just happy to get some nuts. Either way, I was surprised. Later, I asked myself, "Where did this *Gurgle, Gurgle, Gurgle* come from?" I had never heard that sound from him before.

Sparky was still showing signs of a skin disease and it seemed to be getting worse. I questioned myself, "Was the skin disease the result of living in the bottom of the boat with grease, oil, and mildew?"

The next day, I watched a squirrel food fight. No, the squirrels did not throw food at each other like it's shown in the cartoons.

Sparky was eating his usual breakfast of almonds and sunflower seeds in the attic of the squirrel tree house. Another red squirrel was eating sunflower seeds in the bird feeder. All was peaceful, and neither squirrel could see each other. However, I was sure the squirrels could hear each other crack open the sunflower seeds. Then, for some reason, Sparky jumped onto a branch for a better view. Instantly, the other squirrel went on high alert. It turned into a two-minute stare-down with both squirrels standing in fixed and rigid positions. Neither squirrel blinked an eye, made a noise, or moved an inch.

Then, out of the blue, the chase was on. Sparky jumped from his tree and chased the other red squirrel from the bird feeder and up another tree. As I watched, the two squirrels chased each other at high speed through the treetops, screeching the whole time.

The chase lasted another two minutes, and I had no idea if either squirrel caught the other one. But now came the interesting part: both squirrels took a fixed position on a tree branch, and a visual and noisy performance began. Their tails were fully puffed up and were rapidly flickering in the air. Their feet were stomping. Their mouths were spewing all sorts of cackles, screeches, and calls; "*EE-EE, Gurgle-Gurgle, EEEK-EEEK, Chirp-Chirp, Cackle-Cackle, ERRT-ERRT,*" and more.

This stand-off lasted for about ten minutes. It appeared that the noisiest squirrel with the scariest look was the winner. In the end, Sparky went back to his squirrel tree house to finish eating, and slowly, the other red squirrel went back to the bird feeder to finish the sunflower seeds. There was no physical contact. All was peaceful again.

In the end, I do not know what the fight was about. Was it about food? Was it about territory? Or, was this a lover's quarrel with Sparky's new girlfriend. Regardless, every day, the screeching seemed to be more frequent.

Even though I was noticing more red squirrels, at no time did my trail camera pick up more than one red squirrel at a time. Sparky seemed to be the only red squirrel I was able to photograph.

Why do you think squirrels fight?

9

Sparky's Skin Disease Gets Worse

Sparky's skin disease became more apparent and concerning to me. What was I to do? Should I catch Sparky and take him to a veterinarian?

Once again, I turned to Google. I found numerous sites that discussed diseases and health issues regarding squirrels, but I found www.squirrelnutrion.com to be the most informative. Numerous people would post questions, and they would get answered by a caring squirrel lover named William. The site also sold medicine and nutritional food products for squirrels. However, trying to identify

11:07AM 06/04/2021

a skin disease was still a big challenge. Not to mention, how do you give medication to a wild animal? This was a very perplexing problem and I pondered on it for days. I truly thought that without proper care, Sparky would have a very short life.

I even went as far as contacting the squirrel expert himself, William from Squirrel Nutrition and asked if he could help me identify the skin issues; lumpy gray fur on the back shoulders and belly sores. His response was: *"The fur on his bottom is winter fur being shed for a summer coat. Not sure about his belly. Are you sure Sparky is a boy? Because, those spots on the belly look like missing hair around the teats. Sparky may be Sparkette with nursing babies. I can't really get a good look because when I zoom-in it gets fuzzy. If those areas get worse or start looking scabby or bloody, you could always give a dose of Ivermectin just in case it would be mange."*

Well, that statement made me think. Was Sparky a boy or a girl? Was I that wrong for this long of a time frame? The squirrel boy/girl thing was always a struggle for me. You would think they would have made this a little easier for me. I thought all of the photos were of Sparky.

Obviously, I dug out some old photos of Sparky and studied them more closely. Again, to me, Sparky looked like a boy, a very proud boy in fact.

I re-sent some new photos to William, and I asked for his opinion. His response was, *"OK, definitely a better picture. Sparky is a boy!"*

I thought; "What the heck is going on?" I studied more and more pictures. Is this Sparky or is there another squirrel hanging around...Sparkette?

I had absolutely no trail cam photos of two squirrels together in the same picture.

> *How would you deal with Sparky's skin disease? Would you take Sparky to a veterinarian for help?*

10
Surprise! Five Baby Red Squirrels!

Two days later, I found out that **Sparky was a papa** of five baby red squirrels including one runt.

For the last eight weeks, Mrs. Sparky, or now called Sparkette, kept the babies hidden in a large tree about six feet from the infamous Sparky boat. This was a complete surprise to me. It was early morning on Sunday, June 6th, when I discovered the babies.

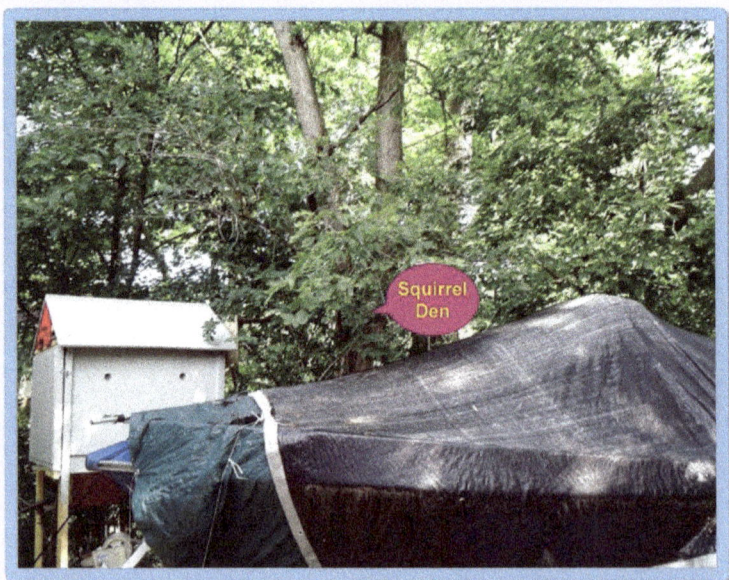

As I walked past the nesting tree, I could hear all of this clicking on the bark of this tree. At first, I saw two small red squirrels, then three, and then four.

I was very surprised!

It was one big playful party of squirrels. I was standing about six feet away and they did not mind me being there at all. Up and down, and around and around they went. It was an endless energy of fun with jumping to no end. This lasted for about an hour, and then, Sparkette must have called them back into the den. Poof! They were gone.

It was amazing to watch only six feet from my sidewalk. I must have walked past that tree fifty times in spring, and I never knew a squirrel nest even existed.

The babies were about eight weeks old; eyes open, fully furred, and with bushy tails. I did not notice the runt until several days later. He had a much smaller tail.

My trail camera never picked up two squirrels at the same time, and it never picked up any baby squirrels. I never even knew Sparky was in a relationship with another squirrel. He had lived in the boat throughout the spring.

I thought, "Wow!, this was a modern-day family!" Sparky had lived in the boat and Sparkette had created a nest in a hollowed out tree six feet next to the boat for the last eight weeks.

I believe Sparky did share the almonds I gave to him on a daily basis, since I saw him jump onto the nesting tree numerous times.

The confusion was finally over, and Sparky was not going to die. He never had a skin disease. All along, Sparkette was the squirrel with the skin issues. I was completely wrong with my observations. The belly sores were the result of Sparkette nursing five very aggressive babies. The lumpy fur on her back must have been related to increased hormone levels.

By coincidence, the squirrel house condo I built was located about six feet from the nesting tree. The real surprise was that I had attached a branch or walkway to the large fork of the tree and the squirrel house condo not knowing there was a squirrel's nest in the tree. I had done this for Sparky's convenience, not for a whole family.

From the very first day Sparky found me, I could never figure out where he was born. I never found a nest. He just appeared at my feet about ten feet from the very same tree. Even today, when I look at the nesting tree, I can't see the hole the squirrels go in and out of. The babies just appear from the large fork in the tree. I figure this must have been the same tree that Sparky's mama and papa used. But, what happened to Sparky's mama and papa?

It was amazing to see how secretive these little creatures can be. I walked past that tree numerous times and had no idea a nest was there. It was only about ten feet off the ground. How could a mother keep five baby squirrels inside that tree for eight weeks? I had trouble managing Sparky for five weeks in a cage inside my house.

Why did Sparky and Sparkette live in separate squirrel nests? How would you hide five baby squirrels for eight weeks?

11
Confusion Resolved

I thought all the trail cam pictures taken during the spring were of Sparky. There was no indication of another squirrel or a nest in a tree right next to Sparky's boat. I only saw two red squirrels chase each other through the trees. In addition, I never saw what a mother squirrel looked like before this event so it never dawned on me there were two squirrels.

Now that my confusion was resolved, I noticed that Sparkette looked very beat up. All along, I truly thought this was Sparky with a skin disease. How could I be so wrong?

I felt sorry for Sparkette, since her body was really being abused by the five babies. About three days after I observed the baby squirrels, I noticed that Sparkette would often lie flat on a branch or in the squirrel tree house attic. She was exhausted.

However, she always kept an eye on her babies. I enjoyed observing her, since she spent hours just lying there. She was cute to watch.

For almost two months, I thought Sparky had contracted some type of skin disease and that his life was going to be cut short. Somehow, nature always seems to surprise me.

I believe the real problem came from the whole process of using a trail cam to document what was happening outside of my house, along with a busy work schedule. The trail cam took hundreds of photographs, and I would select the delete button on an endless basis similar to deleting unwanted e-mails. I would only keep the non-blurry pictures, but I never really analyzed them for detail. If I would have done that, I would have been able to tell there were actually two separate squirrels. I missed it. Also, the batteries went dead in the camera. When I replaced the batteries, the time and date stamp were re-set back to the manufacturing date, which also caused some more confusion.

After going back and looking at the photos more closely, it was easy to see the difference between Sparky and Sparkette.

But now, there were five more squirrels. In another couple of weeks, I would not be able to tell who was who: Sparky, Sparkette, or the Little Sparks.

I continued to monitor Sparkette, and several weeks later, the skin issues seemed to fade away. She looked much better over time.

Sparky

Sparkette

How would you tell the difference between two squirrels?

By their actions and appearance?

By the noises they make?

Using photographs?

Would you have done a better job at identifying Sparky and Sparkette?

12

One Happy Family— Little Sparks Everywhere!

It was a big day for the five baby squirrels. On Monday, June 7th, one day after I noticed them, Sparkette let her babies explore and leave the nesting tree. One after another, they jumped from tree to tree in and out of any tree hole they could find. They even explored Sparky's original tree house and the new squirrel house condo. The babies did not climb higher than fifteen feet, and they did not go further than thirty feet from the nesting tree.

The squirrel house condo became the new romper-room for the babies. I could hear them playing, chasing each other, and grunting with happiness just like Sparky did at that age: "*Grunt, Grunt, Grunt.*"

So once again, I went to the store and bought some blueberries, grapes, and of course, whipped cream. I modified the squirrel house condo by adding a rear porch. I felt Sparkette needed some help weaning the babies off of her and she needed to recover from the bites and scratches caused by the babies.

I was certain that Sparkette would soon be happy, once the babies relied on alternative food sources. This would give her a chance to heal and recover.

I can't begin to imagine how difficult it was for Sparkette to give birth to five babies, in a tree, with the temperature still below freezing, and minimal food. She was required to keep the babies warm for numerous days on end.

It was another big day for the five baby red squirrels. On Tuesday, June 8th, it was all about "How high can you go?"

The whole family, consisting of seven red squirrels, was at the very top of a tall tree next to the nesting tree. It looked as though it was a training exercise with Mom and Dad leading the way. All of the squirrels were chasing each other and playing as a family unit. The branches bent dangerously downward, and amazingly, none of them broke off. I did not see any of the babies fall from the tree. About one hour later, the training exercise spread out to other tree tops within about fifty feet of the nesting tree.

Later, Sparkette and the babies were all tucked away into the nesting tree well before sunset. This was a family that strongly believed in the old saying, "Early to bed, early to rise."

As I thought, reality hit me. I had gone from one orphaned baby red squirrel a year ago to seven red squirrels in one family. What will happen by next year? Will I have twenty to forty red squirrels in my yard?

It was yet another big day for the five baby red squirrels. Thursday, June 10th, was their nighttime training exercise. Just after sunset, one by one, all of the squirrels carefully crawled out of their tree nest. First one head would poke out, then another, and another, to see if it was safe.

A quick check of the neighborhood was followed by a rapid sprint onto the bark of the tree. Finally, the whole family began to run around the nesting tree and soon jumped from branch to branch of other nearby trees. They never went far.

On camera, it looked like Circus Olay (Cirque du Soleil)...running, jumping, flying, spinning, leap frog-ging, and tumbling. Whoops! There it was. I saw a baby squirrel fall to the ground. One by one, the babies made this rather large jump, but the fourth baby missed and headed straight down to the ground. It looked very funny, since all of the other squirrels were moving so fast. None of the other squirrels seemed to care. *What an entertaining act to watch!* Soon everyone was back in the tree hole for an evening head count. The show was all over, and it was time to sleep.

Mornings would start out rather quiet. Not a single red squirrel in sight, just chipmunks. A little time later, one by one, the Little Sparks began to appear. The runt

was usually last out of the hole. I concluded all of the Little Sparks must still be nursing. And, the runt's exit indicated breakfast was over. Almonds and sunflower seeds did not appear to be their number-one priority. The babies were all about play. The Little Sparks seemed to be happy with exploring each branch and jumping from tree to tree. They did not appear to be in any hurry, since they would stop and sit in the usual cute round position, and just watch the chipmunks and other animals.

Once in a while, two or more Little Sparks would chase and wrestle with each other, no matter how high up they were in the tree. On another occasion, I did see two of the babies wrestle with each other, and one of them fell about eight feet to the ground hitting other branches on the

way down. The baby shook it off and climbed right back into the tree.

Most mornings were very peaceful and the Little Sparks were fun to watch. However, once the gray squirrels and blue jays stopped by for a snack, the silence was broken by numerous danger dances, screeches, and cackles.

Sparkette must have heard all the noises from within the den and finally poked her head out. She would fly out of the den, jump on the boat, and say, *"Chip, Chip, Chip."* (Time to take charge) Her chase was on. First, the chipmunks were chased away. Then she would go after the gray squirrels, which were a little more difficult. The blue jays were next. However, for Sparkette, the blue jays were impossible to scare off. The Sparky family just had to ignore the blue jays, and let the small sparrow bird group dive bomb them until they left the area.

Once Sparkette had the neighborhood back in control, she would wonder, *"Where is my food?"*

Even though Sparkette was still nursing her babies and she was out of shape, she still had plenty of energy to command the neighborhood. It was impressive to watch. Once she finished her breakfast of almonds and sunflower seeds, the Little Sparks would clean up the rest of the food. This usually turned into a lot of squabbling, tumbling, chasing, and gibberish name calling.

You might ask, "Where was Sparky?" "Where did he sleep?" Those are both good questions.

Sparky would come and go. He was not as involved with the Little Sparks as Sparkette, but he was always nearby. I think he was more involved with the training exercises like; treetop jumping, and late-night stealth and safety climbing. I do not know where he slept.

Within two weeks of leaving the den, the Sparky family would now take day trips. One by one, they would leave my yard. I would not see them for the rest of the day. My guess was that the whole family left to find some cooler temperatures in the nearby pine trees.

In the evening, I would see them return one by one. I would look up and see a trail of little red squirrels jumping through the treetops. Once they were back in my yard, water, almonds and sunflower seeds were the first priority. Soon after that, the fighting began, *"Er, Er, Er, Er."*

In the morning hours on the day after one of their extended day trips, the Sparky family would sleep in until around 9:00 a.m. Does this sound familiar in comparison to your family?

Shortly after several family trips, the Little Sparks explored the neighborhood on their own. Sparky and Sparkette stayed behind. Sparkette would lie flat on her belly to rest and recover. On certain occasions, she didn't even care if I placed some food right next to her. She was extremely tired.

Do squirrel families stay together or do the baby squirrels go their separate ways?

13

The Little Sparks Grow Up Fast

There is little room in the wild for a baby animal. Red and gray squirrels must grow up fast. If not, game over!

Sparky and Sparkette were very quick to teach their babies how to make it on their own. This included a strange meal-sharing program. Every morning, Sparkette wouldn't share her almonds or sunflower seeds. She would let her babies know this with a soft, "*Er, Er, Er, Er*" (Don't touch, this is my food. Find your own.)

Within ten days, the babies were weaned off of milk, and they were now fully self-reliant and independent squirrels. This was difficult for me to believe, since it had taken me five weeks after Sparky's release before he became completely self-reliant and independent. Maybe I babied him too much. Maybe I was a bad teacher. Or, maybe I was just not a good surrogate mother.

The Sparky tree house seemed to become the central location during the day. The babies came and went as they pleased. They were free to do whatever they wanted to. Sparkette just hung out and watched from a distance. There was never any scolding or funny noises being made while Sparkette watched her babies.

In addition, I felt as though I was being watched by seven sets of eyeballs while working in my yard or driveway. On a few occasions, one of the squirrels would perform a *"Danger Dance"* when I entered their space.

Also, on several occasions, a large bird would land in the nearby trees. Then my yard would come alive with all types of chirps, squeaks, and *ERRT*s. It was high alert for everyone, including squirrels, chipmunks, and other birds. I could not tell what type of bird it was, but it definitely created a stir.

Sparkette would put her babies on notice, and all of the playing would come to a complete stop. The high alert would last for about twenty minutes until the large bird would leave.

Sparkette appeared to be recovering nicely. She was now weaning the babies off of her milk, and I saw the babies eat other types of food. Whipped cream was again a big hit with the babies and Sparkette. I did not see Sparky eat any whipped cream this time, but I am sure he did when I wasn't looking.

To date, the squirrel house condo was a success. Oftentimes, I would hear the babies rummaging around inside; wrestling, fighting for food, playing hide and seek, and squabbling over who gets what bedroom. However, after seeing the size of the family, I wondered if I had made the squirrel house condo big enough. I thought, "Will they all live there?"

The baby red squirrels appeared to grow up much faster with a natural family than with just one surrogate mother. After watching the babies for a week and a half, I could no longer call them babies. Their training appears to be complete, of which fifty percent came from playing with siblings, and fifty percent came from Sparky and Sparkette.

The young squirrels were now acting like a group of individuals exploring the area and searching for food on a daily basis. They would still join together during the day by chance, or to share a family meal with a lot of "*Err,*

Err, Err, Err." Sparky and Sparkette's efficiency at raising their young was amazing.

It was now three weeks since the baby red squirrels first popped their heads out of the nesting tree. Sparkette appears to have recovered nicely from the strenuous task of nursing and raising five babies. Her sores healed, the inflammation subsided, but she still had some gray fur on her back shoulders. All seven of the red squirrels were the same size and they all looked alike.

Throughout the baby-raising process, Sparkette seemed to accept me rather well. I normally had my hand within six inches of her when I was placing almonds in the squirrel tree house. Often times, Sparkette would just lie on her belly in the attic of the squirrel tree house with her head hanging over the edge as she just watched me climb the ladder or work in the driveway.

One evening, I think I ran across Sparky. He came to the squirrel tree house and again he was acting all giddy and playful. He ran back and forth on the branches nearest to me. He had a bounce in his step that I had never seen before. He kept watching me. I think this time it was his way of saying "Hello" to an old friend.

After the enthusiastic greeting, it was back to normal; "*Hey, feed me! Where are my almonds?*"

When he was done eating, off he went.

14

Sparky, It's Time to Reclaim My Boat!

In early July, I proceeded to clean out my boat. There were no surprises to me, but many people would be amazed at how much stuff one squirrel could accumulate in just five months. I just didn't have the heart to kick Sparky out sooner.

Damage Report! One hole in the floor, one severed wire, and a wheelbarrow full of trash.

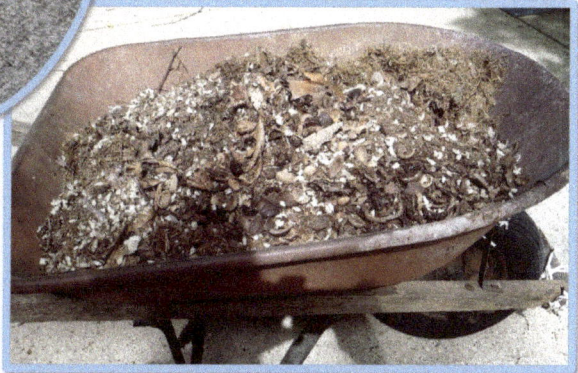

15

Why Is My Yard So Quiet?

It was the morning of July 5th and there were no red squirrels, gray squirrels, chipmunks, or birds in sight. I asked myself, "Was this quiet the result of a noisy 4th of July weekend or some other reason?" It was very unusual not to see chipmunks. They all must have been hiding.

However, I remembered that during the evening of July 4th, I had observed two baby owls about ten feet away from me. They were sitting on a railing about four feet high in my back yard. I think they were just learning how to fly and remained visible for about fifteen minutes. Fireworks were going off in the background and it was completely dark.

I thought, "This is odd. I have never seen any owls in my yard, much less two baby owls. Had they been frightened by the fireworks?"

The following day, I thought to myself, "This can't be a good thing. I had a family of baby squirrels in the front yard and a family of baby owls in the back yard." Owls have been known to eat small animals like squirrels and chipmunks.

For weeks, I did not see any squirrels, gray or red. I think my yard became a potential food buffet for the owls, although I never saw the owls eat anyone.

By chance or by natural instinct, the squirrels had decided to leave the area. Or, maybe they were searching for better food, cooler weather, attractive mates, or just out exploring. Whatever the reason, I would never know.

It was now September and still no squirrels. I only saw a few gray squirrels collecting nuts during harvest season. My yard was nothing compared to the squirrel activity just one year ago. I thought, "Maybe there is some type of squirrel gathering taking place somewhere else."

My yard had been pretty much empty with the exception of a few chipmunks since the middle of July. The predator birds and owls must have scared everyone away.

October came around and I had not seen any red squirrels for several months. Then out of the blue, I heard two red squirrels squabbling in the squirrel house condo. It sounded like Sparky and Sparkette. There was no food in the squirrel house condo so I did not know what they were fighting about. However, after some thought, I could only imagine that the argument was about future living accommodations.

Sparky was saying; "But I like it here. It is a big house with many rooms and easy-to-find almonds." Sparkette was saying; "I don't like the flooring, the windows are all wrong, the curtains are the wrong color, and I don't like your friend. Your friend keeps calling you Sparky. Your real name is (#!*@Jibberish@$%^)."

After about ten minutes of squabbling, Sparky and Sparkette ran out of the squirrel house condo and disappeared into the trees, never to be seen together again.

After about a year and a half of following Sparky, I thought the story has finally come to an end. My mistake.

Surprise! Sparky was back.

It was now the middle of November, eighteen months after Sparky initially found me, and the little red squirrel had begun to hang around again. This time, he moved into the squirrel house condo I had made, six feet away from last year's nesting tree. This was crazy.

The little red squirrel was once again collecting nuts, pine cones, leaves, grass, and pine needles, and placing them in the squirrel house condo. He was once again living the good life as a bachelor. I know it was Sparky because I would place several fleece strips outside every

day and they would disappear over night. No other squirrel had ever touched the fleece strips. Over time, I cut up a queen-sized mattress pad into two-inch fleece strips, and placed them in the attic of the squirrel house condo. Within a month, the mattress pad was completely cut up and the fleece strips were all gone. *What a character!* Thank goodness he was not loading up my boat this time.

I saw Sparky almost daily, but he no longer came up to me. Most of the time, he either ran into the squirrel house condo or into the hollowed-out nesting tree from last year. A few times, he started his crazy *"Danger Dance"* thing, which meant I should leave. Winter was just around the corner.

What will the inside of the squirrel house condo look like in spring?

Nature can be very interesting, but you have to slow down, listen, and watch. My investment of some time, a few almonds, and maybe four cans of whipped cream was definitely worth the journey. In return, I was able to cross the line and have a short-term friendship with a wild animal. I watched Sparky go through a full lifecycle from baby to papa.

While sharing my experience with you, I am sure the two-book series of "Sparky & Me" made you smile at least once.

Enjoy the outdoors!

Whoops! I was wrong again.

It was the middle of December, and I noticed two red squirrels living in and around the squirrel house condo. I heard no squabbling. I saw no wild chases through the trees. I just saw two red squirrels trying to cope with each other and navigate through the cold winter months.

Sparky and Sparkette must have come to an agreement about where to live.

Where will this story end?

How would you pronounce Sparky's real name in squirrel language?

Fun Photos

Your guess is as good as mine. Is this chipmunk Long Tail, Bushy Tail, Short Tail, or Broken Tail? Can s/he get any more food in his/her mouth?

Sparky and Me II

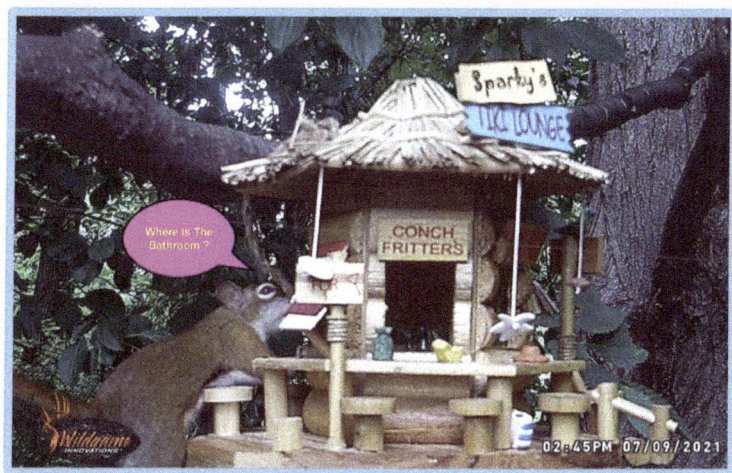

67

Sparky and Me II

Closing Remarks from the Author

This book is meant to inspire people to respect nature. Sometimes nature needs our help. And, by no means is this book meant to inspire the capture or poaching of any wild animal as a pet. More specifically, this book is not intended to promote the cutting down of trees to obtain a squirrel as a pet.

Again, squirrels do not make good pets. They belong in the wild with their family and friends. My encounter with Sparky was a rare and unexpected occurrence. There are numerous wildlife-in-need shelters across the nation, which are standing by ready to help if you are unable to care for an injured or orphaned wild animal on your own.

Years ago, I would feed the birds and chase the squirrels away from the bird feeder. Now, after meeting Sparky, I feed the squirrels and I find myself chasing the blue jays away. WOW! Have I changed! Just remember all wild animals need to eat, not just the ones you like.

Finally, children should not try to touch or pet wild squirrels. The little animals can get scared and possibly bite. Just remember the "*ERRRT, ERRRT, ERRRT,*" and "*EEK, EEK, EEK*" from the first book, *Sparky and Me*. Sparky was not a pet. He was a wild animal, and I had to be careful when dealing with him at all times.

References and Credits

www.squirrelnutrition.com

Special thanks to:

Hildegard Meissner
Cindy Musbach
Judy Reinders

In Memory Of:

Joanne Minessale

About the Author

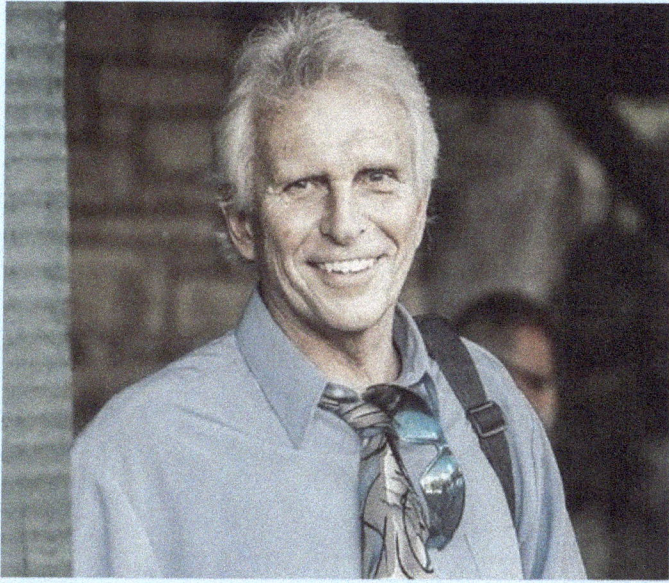

Richard Meissner attended the University of Wisconsin-Milwaukee and Marquette University, and graduated with his Bachelor's and Graduate degrees in Business Administration and Accounting. Currently, Richard is a self-employed tax and accounting business professional located in southeast Wisconsin. Richard enjoys the outdoors and nature in his spare time. Richard's house was built on a wooded lot with many trees, and is located on Lake Keesus, Merton, WI. Accordingly, small wild animals are very common to see.

For over thirty years, Richard has cared for and helped numerous wild animals including snapping turtles, painter turtles, raccoons, rabbits, fish, birds, and deer, but never a squirrel. This was a first for Richard. And, quite the enjoyable challenge it was. After reading the book, you might think that it almost sounds like a movie, *"One Man and a Baby Squirrel—He is Nuts, Nuts, Nuts."*

The wild animals living around Richard's house must know that they are safe when Richard is around. Obviously, that is why Sparky chose Richard for help, and adopted Richard to be his surrogate mother. Richard is a very creative thinker, and he enjoys working with his hands. Therefore, solutions to problems are easy for Richard, such as building temporary squirrel tree houses, and later remodeling them as the need arises.

"Nuts, Nuts, Nuts."

www.ingramcontent.com/pod-product-compliance
Lightning Source LLC
Chambersburg PA
CBHW051431270326
41934CB00018B/3478